'I AM' EXPERIMENTS

SEARCH FOR HEALING AND SELF REALIZATION IN INDIAN YOGIC SYSTEM

SUKHENDU MANDAL
PHD

ISBN 979-888546289-1

ॐ नमः शिवाय

Contents

FOREWORD

Prof. Subrata Sau, Senior Scientist Bose Institute, Kolkata

The author has discovered something that could bring together Science and Spirituality at the same time appeal to the new generation to connect with the inherent wisdom from the Yogic systems.

This book has a unique type of information that integrates science with spirituality.

Sukhendu was a PhD student under my guidance working in the field of DNA protein interaction in Staphylococcus. After submission of his PhD thesis, he happens to disappear from the lab and the world of Molecular research. I believed he has left the research field and was up to something else. Later I received updates about his writing project and upcoming books.

During the last meeting, I got the privilege to attend his seminar on the topic of Healing Codes. I always knew him as shy and not so interested in speaking up. But this seminar was different, he has transformed into a vibrational speaker. His words create some type of subtle vibrations as he shares his knowledge.

There were other scientists in the seminar and some of them made similar remarks. The vibrations and subtle energy continued for days after the meet and it created changes in mental and emotional levels.

This work may have powerful application in Neuroscience research and equally uplifting to the society.

I

Discernment

> *"Mastery is knowing what to take and what to ignore."*

The concepts and level of spiritual work shared in this book needs a deep level of dedication and practice. The reader must be a mature adult well aware of personal responsibilities.

The author has tried a search for a universal philosophy that could uplift every aspect of life. In practical reality, there is no Universal philosophy that would apply to everyone and all aspects of life. Because personal philosophies shape every aspect of life and choices, applying spiritual philosophies to practical life might be pretty misleading. Reader's discernment is essential.

Discernment is one of the powerful concepts from the first book in this series. It allows a person to try different concepts and beliefs without being lost in the flow.

Get inspired, feel free to try new beliefs and philosophies. If it doesn't feel right, it's not the right thing.

Move on.

Some points to consider:

1. All stories and information is personal point of view.
2. Do not confuse self care for self medication.
3. The term healing is not used in reference of medical cure.
4. When in need of directions seek a right mentor specialized in the particular field.
5. Wrong rituals may lead to distortion of beliefs and sense of self causing a gap in skills development and connection with reality.
6. Spirituality is a dimension of metaphors. It may not entirely connect with practical reality.
7. At times the information may be misleading for some people or age groups.

The tools and techniques are for personal clarification (thoughts, emotions, beliefs, values) and not for therapeutic purpose.

II

A word with the Author

> *"It is only average quality delivered when one person does everything."*

Receiving feedback from readers and experts, I realized the first book missed something important; the story of the author.

The focus was so much on writing a technique-centered book that it missed the point that book readers pick a book on authenticity from a credible source irrespective of the type of information shared.

So as not to miss the vital point of credibility, this book has my story, research background, and source of inspiration for writing.

The first book also had some technical errors that only the Authors would recognize. It has much content written in First Person. And because I received multiple messages from readers that they enjoyed the writing, there was no reason to edit it.

Ultimately, the writing was to be focused on the reader's taste.

Selling self as Credible Source of Information

There has been some advice to be a credible source and offer the information about self to the readers before they can trust the work. The most important advice was to share my story. By then, the first book was sent for editing. Story addition might need restructuring the entire book.

So the content was made into a separate book covering the later part of the project.

Tell me About yourself

The first interview I was ever asked to tell me about myself in 60 seconds, I told them everything. And I witnessed one of the interviewers slap his forehead and secretly smile.

I did the same in writing until I learned some basic copywriting skills.

What type of Person Am I

A person who still pronounces Charisma as Cha-rishma, has unique lyrics to every song and likes to live far from the cities. I recently realized there is also a strong sense of imposter syndrome when writing about self. Generally known to be silent guy except for a few unlucky ones.

Education

I was always interested in the experimental field and trying out new things. I took up Biotechnology as an opportunity to go into the research. Graduation to Doctorate I continued in Biotechnology. The doctorate research project was on molecular microbiology.

I once happen to say DNA work as my field of research in a seminar whereby later someone asked me to teach them DNA work. I realized later that DNA work is an esoteric technique, and the person confused lab research with metaphysical work.

I had zero background in metaphysical research. There is no relationship between my PhD research and the book writings. It was out of interest I began writing in this field, then got in the flow of finding unique information.

I decided to try Neuroscience in the next part of my research career.

The pandemic struck right in time and delayed everything.

Luckily, I could manage the writings with limited resources, an old computer, and little to no editorial support.

Spiritual Background

In a country like India, there is no need to get certified to have a spiritual background. The family teachings themselves has a high level of spiritual education.

Parents and grandparents taught the first of the mantra chantings and meditation. Living a spiritual discipline was part of daily aesthetics. People these days seem to attend paid workshops to learn these habits, which were ingrained from a young age.

The only extra tool I had from others was being taught kundalini yoga at the age of 11. It was introduced in a martial arts camp, and I took it up to master Kung-Fu and someday being able to catch a bullet like the Kung-fu masters. I spent years practising meditation, which I now know is a simple form of focus and does not have anything with stopping a bullet.

But yes, that was it. The kundalini meditation has made me quite sensitive and brought more trouble than good in the years.

For some reason, extra sensitivity attracts more bullying, abuse and attacks. It also caused terms of sadness and depression due to involvement with other's problems.

Hobbies

Collecting old coins and currencies was a full-time hobby since my school days. I travelled to places in the hope of finding some historic coins and collectables. This hobby has a special connection with this work. It will be clear with the later chapters.

I also read a lot during the college days. The last was trying my hands on guitar, which to date, I hardly could pick a tune on the strings.

Lately, I got interested in collecting meteorites and some rare crystals to add to my collection.

When I moved to writing and launched the project Beyond Placebo, I needed to sell everything to fund the project.

Alternative Medicine

I did study a lot of alternative medicine systems, but that was all from books. There is no practical background. During the writing process, I spent more than a year with a Senior consultant and hypnotherapist, learning about the subconscious mind and its abilities.

I also attended workshops in multiple modalities to learn about energy healing. I interacted with dozens of healers and coaches, experienced sessions in numerous healing modalities, and have gone through few thousands of metadata corrections.

Spiritual Energy sensitivity

When you go to a workshop, it is easy to experience healing techniques through a trainer. But the experience and induction generally get dissolved in a few days. Even the books written by the founder of specific techniques emit subtle vibrations. This entirely depends on the background of the author and the information they share.

Being able to sense the space and vibrating all the time began after a long term sickness. I turned out so sensitive that even a mild change would cause me to feel it.

Until I could feel it myself, I was sceptical of any existence of yogic techniques and any spiritual knowledge.

This turned out to be my radar in this project and the inspiration to continue.

Beyond Placebo Channel

The channel was launched in 2019 to introduce the concepts of the project in the pre-release phase. With hardly any skills, the channel began with 1-minute slides like videos explaining the idea of codes. The first few viewers took it for a healing meditation and expected a more extended version of music to relax.

Longer music sessions were shared with later videos, but this changed the concept of codes to healing music meditation. A new form of healing system was discovered that viewers found much more effective than the book's healing codes.

This day the channel has more than 200 different healing sessions designed with free music and healing codes.

The most practical explanation about music sessions being much more effective than the healing codes would be that music sessions keep the mind aware of healing. Another esoteric explanation is that music is much more physical and tangible than intentional words, so it has a more profound effect.

Hobby to Authorship

I was inspired into writing as early as 2008-09, but the writing began in bits in pieces from 2012. I didn't realize the challenges until I bought the first publishing contract in 2019. Till then, I was in the air about writing and becoming a published author.

The only aim was to complete one book and submit it before PhD award. There was no sight of taking this work further.

This was going to be more serious than expected.

But, the morning I received the mail from Publishers, and I was to submit it within 90 days. A contract was to be signed plus a complete detailed list of information needed to submit a book plus later promotions.

There were a few dozen things on the list I had no idea about. It felt like being trapped in the wrong place and wrong time with a 90 days limit. I couldn't help but panic.

Trying to take hold of the situation and having no idea where to start, I called one of the mentors (NLP Coach) for directions. I tried my best to hold onto the anxiety.

The only answer I received was "work on one thing at a time".

This one-thing-at-a-time extended till 2021, when the first book was released. The publisher's contract was kept pending because the to-do list could not be fulfilled in time.

Writing Skills

When the writing began in a serious mode and with a time limit, all other issues raised their heads. The first was the structure of the book. Outlining took away my sleep for days.

Then the disaster struck in. At some point, you will need to scale your writing skill to decide the type of editing you will need and seek a professional editor.

My writing skill was a total disaster to be 1 on a scale of 1-10. There is no way I was meant to be a writer.

The steaming journey of a writer to an author is now a distant dream.

Structural issues, linguistic gaps, grammatical errors and lacking flow were peak issues with many other problems.

And there was no source of money to fund the editor.

Dividing into four major structures

The first draft of writing has multiple concepts and a cluttered feeling. It does not seem to be a complete manuscript. Most non-fiction books focused on only one idea, and the outline directs all information to the core concept.

So, the outline of the book was divided into four and named the Beyond Placebo project.

Now the major trouble was being able to write an entire book on a single topic.

What I always avoided in exams was long questions and, at times, would skip a question and lose marks just to avoid lengthy writings.

And here I am, facing it again.

Monetary Problems

The last salary I received was in 2017, and all saving has been exhausted. Two out of three instalments for the book contract were paid by friends and some well-wishers from seminars. I was expecting to refund the money within few months.

But there were all the other unknown expenses soon to show up that I wasn't prepared for.

To save funds, a large part of non-author work was taken care of by myself, from getting a website to all SEO, creating and maintaining social media accounts on 12 different platforms, creating a channel, buying needed applications for deciding the title of book etc.

It is only average quality delivered when one person takes care of everything. But this was only the boot camp.

It took atleast a year of training to understand editing and copywriting, SEO for website and channel, optimizing the title of a book for visibility, copywriting for ads and book description. By this time, the channel has grown to 2000+ subscribers, and it is now eligible as the promotion page along with a website.

Seeking Experts

I tried to cut off on all expenses in this period. There were no travels or tours for almost two years, no shopping, no eating outside, plus no paying for any services.

The first book was ready by the end of December and needed a proper cover. I took help from one of my cousins with artistic skills to design the cover. The ebook was released just before Christmas.

There were some sales, mainly from the channel. In a week, I realized this book is not going to work because of its cover. Cover making is not a skill for the author.

The book cover was updated along with the release of the paperback.

No one buys new authors

The new cover received a better response than earlier. But the sales were still meagre and reach only an income of 2000rs per month which is not enough to pay the electric bill. At the same time, the debt in the process happened to be more than a lakh. It needed atleast 10,000 copies to be sold before the entire expense on this project is procured.

Visibility

If not for the debt and need for income, I must have experienced a great sense of achievement. There was a lot I learned in the process.

But now, success means conversion. The need to pay back was pressing by as two months passed with few sales. During the release month, there were some sales, and then it dropped to 4-6 copies a month.

Something has to be done.

Promotions and marketing on a limited budget is nothing but an illusion. All this money fall in the dark spots in the market—a space where there is zero response at all.

I had learned about all the ways of promotions and took every service I could afford. There were thousands of downloads during the free promotions whereby I needed to pay for the marketing, but the book has to be free for readers. There was no positive effect from the promotions, neither in sales nor in reviews.

The fine line

As per the reviews from good sources, the book has been successful, but the promotions have failed. All the promotions and returns were in the fine line where there was a loss of revenue.

It would be much cheaper to send free copies to people than spend on services.

Entrepreneurship

An author is a misfit in the marketing world. Thinking like one no more helps with the situation. There were new levels of skills and mindset needed.

Am I supposed to be happy to be a published author, or do I take responsibility to be a successful author?

I am still in the process of working out the situation.

The doubt and debt continues for now.

III
Introduction

"The mind sees only what it wants to see and believes only what it wants to believe."

A deep need for a higher purpose inspired the search for meaning in Indian yogic systems. A research student's perception of ancient yogic knowledge created a unique information template that would transform and awaken anyone who would like to connect with the information.

A new design to the spiritual secrets from the sacred land of India that could be applied to all aspects of life. It is shared with exciting stories and a powerful collection of philosophies that create spontaneous transformation and healing.

At times, the flow might sound non-linear; in such cases, the story must be part of a healing session that surfaced the inner programs. Most stories are unrelated to each other but have a specific lesson that ultimately structured the entire process. Some stories may not make sense at the time, while some may give a 'Wow' moment of relating and self-realization.

Some philosophies from this work might go a long way in transforming every aspect of life. Some might inspire new ones.

Let this book spark that Transformational Philosophy you already hold.

Signals from life

The human mind is in constant interaction with everything creating an exemplary feedback system. There is a continuous stream of signals every moment. All one needs to do is tune-up in the circuit.

Small events and experiences in everyday life may signal inherent patterns and subconscious programs creating issues in life. These signals start long before any major problem shows up in life. Some stories shared in this book have to do with identifying the signs.

The Idea Beyond Placebo

The name of the project was decided with years of discussions in research groups. Because every concept of ancient medicine would fairly end in the Placebo effect, there was no meaning in trying a Re-search for the same thing.

What I experienced was much more than a placebo effect.

The name was spontaneous.

Struggles in a Project

I had no idea where, to begin with. All I wanted to study was the science behind spiritual beliefs in this country. It began as simple as checking the sound note from temple bells with guitar tuning apps to asking people who knew about ancient medicine. Even asking a monk to show the spiritual dimension whereby the answer was, "if you need a teacher like Paramhansa, then become a student like Vivekananda."

Planning

Many stories said, if you search the sacred sites in India, there are chances you will find old scriptures that have concepts of ancient medicines. So I was planning to travel to the south and visit all sacred sites searching for some scriptures.

There were all types of plans, to begin with.

None ever executed.

A fair warning

After considering my idea of ancient medicine, one of the well-wishers said, "For now, do not leave your research field. This spiritual medicine system has already ruined someone's career."

It is sure a space designed on quicksand.

The mythologies and local belief systems sound so alluring, but the outcome is a waste of time and resources when taken to lab research.

Why?

If science is not advanced enough? If spiritual stories are fake?

The answer is both and neither.

There is a massive gap between what is being propagated in collective beliefs and what is actually possible on a human scale. At the same time, the research methods were not meant for this type of system. And research proposals cannot be made based on personal beliefs.

Pitfalls

With dozens of direct interactions over a few years, I realized what sounds like a world of spiritual consciousness is much more distorted and has no connection with practical reality.

Supernatural events happen now and then in various places that attract large masses of devotees, but most of these events have nothing to do with supernatural or even higher consciousness.

The mind so much engaged and invested in religion tends to see everything as a miracle. All it goes was a waste of time and energy. Seeking things with great expectations to end up with distortions.

A large part of spirituality falls in this space.

Those who have a genuine connection to this knowledge and wisdom seem to be inaccessible or non-existent for the time.

Source of all this Information

The sources of all information were local legends, stories, interaction with people, local culture and rituals, asking a lot of other coaches, authors and healers. Another source of information was from books but limited.

One piece of information sometimes took weeks to months for proper understanding and integration.

The information that reached the point of practical application has been shared with others through writings and seminars. The feedback has been the most essential part of the work for refining the information.

Information that was found to be impractical was cut off and removed.

This is how bits and pieces of practical information were collected over years before it was set into a proper structure of a book.

Because no part of this information was fit to go into research material, the idea to write a research project or review was dropped and kept limited to publishing books to bring the information into the public domain.

This book will give a clear picture of how the information was collected and how it was deciphered as something applicable to body-mind-emotional wellness.

IV

Pilgrimage to Sacred Sites

"Mind perceives reality in structures."

All the information shared about the topic originated from people, yogis, and local legends. An integrated form of the information is shared in this chapter. There could be other possibilities that are not covered here.

Tirtha or Sacred Sites

There needs to be a transparent and fair definition of a sacred site to discuss the topic further.

In India, there are 100s of 1000s of places known to be of religious value to people. Every year millions of people travel to these places to receive divine blessings and grace. Hindu families have the tradition to travel and visit the significant tirtha places atleast once in life. Those who cannot cover all of them try to visit atleast some of them.

Why has it been so important to visit a particular place to receive divine grace? The divine consciousness is present everywhere, so what is the role of these places?

The answer varies from person to person. But there must be some vital aspect not very well known to the commoner.

Probably, the answer lies in those sites. Or there must be someone who could answer that is free of relative perception and distortions of logic.

How the Sacred Sites are formed

As described by a Yogi from a certain rare sect in India, a place where a spiritual master takes Samadhi has intense spiritual energies. The exact site where the master practiced meditation has to be closed and kept safe from people. The reason for guarding the site was to keep people safe from absorbing the intense level of spiritual energies that the place has. Not every person is ready to handle the amount of energy a yogi achieves in years of meditation. The seekers are kept at a distance from the place. Those prepared for the initiations in the path of self-realizations easily receive it, while those not ready get least affected.

This answers one of the queries that most sacred sites developed due to a spiritual master living their life in a specific place and working in their path of self-realization. The place has the energies from the person even after centuries passed. Most sacred sites are later followed by generations of disciples from the same spiritual master, and the lineage of spiritual work continued for ages in that place.

There is another theory of sacred sites believed in the west. Also, some temples in India talk about it on the theory of Parikrama- why we go round the temple only in a specific direction. It is believed that the earth has multiple high energy spots that have a natural flow of higher dimensional energies. Due to their high energy levels, these places support a robust level of spiritual development and activations. So most sacred sites are naturally formed in these places. Spirituals and seekers all around the world are naturally attracted to these places for their spiritual development.

Spiritual Evolution

The only part of spiritual work that a human has control over is purification. Everything else is said to be natural and in control of the Higher consciousness. From the ordinary person's perspective, spiritual evolution would be a level of clarity and purity in mind, body, and emotions.

But there is much more happening at energetic levels. Spiritual evolution begins after a certain level of maturity is achieved on mental and emotional levels. There are no signs or ways to measure a person's spiritual development.

The yogic system describes a soul's spiritual evolution through seven levels of activations. Some explain it in terms of seven chakras blooming.

It takes years or even decades to complete one initiation at a time. Some people go through parallel levels, while some stay stuck with one level. The only thing a person has in control is the choice to learn and grow. As the lessons integrate, new levels of activations happen.

Because these are natural processes, every human goes through them and completes the primary initiations without any spiritual background. Those working on mastering their mind and emotions also process through the major initiations.

The later higher initiations needed support from the higher consciousness and spiritual teachers.

Spiritual Work at Sacred Sites

The sacred sites have the vibrational space to maintain the high spiritual energy needed for spiritual activations. It is easier to receive, hold and integrate a much higher level of energy in these places. Most spiritual seekers engage in deep spiritual work or sacred rituals in these sites. Also, many seekers find their spiritual guru to receive their activation in the path of Initiations.

People express a significant shift in consciousness, a state of joy and freedom, a deeper connection with life, and a natural flow during and after the tirtha (visit to the sacred site).

Every Site is Unique

Though the seeker's intention is the same, the spiritual process followed in all places is similar, and so the fruit of tirtha must be; but every site is said to be unique. People follow a particular pattern when visiting multiple sites across India. Each site is said to have a unique vibration and purpose in spiritual evolution. Also, it is said most of these sites are energetically connected. Visiting the sites in a particular sequence has levels of activations in consciousness that otherwise would not happen in only one location.

Some sites feel serene and peaceful, while there are sites that are intense and amplifying.

Trying to determine the millions of yogis this country has seen, there could be as many templates of spiritual initiations already imprinted in the sacred sites around this country alone.

Tune-up in the energy of the Sacred Sites

The time spent in the place allows an initiate to receive as much conscious flow of spiritual energy and consciousness. Also, there is a certain amount of time needed to integrate these energies before the shift in consciousness shows up in the behavior and attitude of a person.

Some sacred sites have a major level of spiritual consciousness, and then there are many minor levels sites branched out from the main site. Every primary site resonates with all the other sites on earth and aligns with the higher dimensional energy grid that connects the earth to the Consciousness of the Universe.

Due to their vast pool of information and energies, the major sites allow some major level of spiritual activations. Also, these sites allow expansion of any initiate's spiritual field, which otherwise stays limited to the mental field. This expanded form of energetic field allows a direct connection with Higher consciousness and tune-up with universal energies. This field is called Lightbody. Once the lightbody activates, it continues to expand through the integration of consciousness to all sacred energy connections on earth. It then ascends to the Solar level and then further to the Universal level. This happens after the Samadhi of the initiate and the activation of this lightbody anchors the universal energies in the Place the Yogi takes Samadhi. This place develops as another sacred site.

Temples and Sacred Geometries

Almost all temples follow a certain vedic design of construction. There could be designs and symbols found in every temple. These designs and symbols are not just art structures. They follow the principles of spiritual initiations.

The temple itself is designed in the form of a lightbody to anchor the higher spiritual energies. This is one reason, it feels so peaceful and conscious when being inside a temple.

The symbols and geometries have another purpose not quite accessible for the common man or even beginner initiates.

There are temples in India where the primary site of reverence has only one major design. These designs and geometries have their spiritual significance and activate the flow of consciousness when interacted with. But the activation is only possible by someone ready to receive it.

These symbols are the keys to higher levels of consciousness. Most of these symbols are developed by yogis with years of spiritual work, and the symbol anchors the blueprint of their spiritual consciousness.

What the Ancient Yogis left behind for Us

India has been a habitat for millions of yogis and seekers. Some of them are highly attained in the path of self-realization. It is said that the field of spiritual energy and information stays forever once created by a realized one. This created a vast pool of spiritually rich information all around the country, especially at sacred sites where most yogis lived their lives.

Then there were some who decided to leave a legacy of spiritual teachings and practices through their lineage of disciples.

There were also those who created special techniques and tools like mantras, mudras, kriyas, and meditation techniques.

There were others who left behind signs and symbols of sacred resonance for the later generations.

This book series was inspired by several interactions with this rich knowledge of spirituality.

Each system is Unique

The most common form of worship practiced in India is Idol worship. But there are other forms seen.

Some temples have ancient mantras, design, or symbol that is worshiped. Then there are also some rare places where the worship site is empty and devoid of any material form. These places worship the formless without any particular ritual.

V

Let the Journey Begin

"Life is a larger cycle of our tiny Patterns."

Jazmin

The slide

I was in grade 3 when I learned this lesson the hard way. But the pattern continues.

It was a school picnic at a nearby park. As the bus reached, the elders moved to sightsee while the children rushed to the park.

I was excited by the distant view of this new park, especially the giant slide.

To date, I didn't experience a slide. It seems fun on television.

There is no time to waste.

I needed to try it out. It must be real fun!

While other children dispersed around the place, claiming their place to play, I climbed the metal stairs and was ready to slide.

The next moment, I was on the ground and hit my head on the edge of the steel plate.

Shocked for a few moments with no injury.

I avoided the slide for the next part of our stay in that town.

It was no fun, mere disaster.

Our family shifted to another place, and I got into a new school. This school has its double slides and merry-go-round.

The class fellows are more in tune with the slides. They would slide off-on, sideways, counter and standing.

With them, I learned the new skill to slide and control the speed of Slippery slopes.

Well, one needs some skills even to have fun!!!

Years passed by, I still have the same patterns to jump onto anything and everything, meet a disaster and then avoid it for some time till some skilled ones show up.

The Damage

I looked into my plate, and it was empty.

How so!

There was supposed to be a sweet in it.

I looked to the right, and there was a big mouth gobbling my food and smirking like a retard.

So the favourite food is gone.

Looked left; there was already a strong defence around the plate.

No way of getting it.

Walking out of the hall to discard my plate, I saw someone munching on her food.

No defence around the plate.

I stepped closer as she smiled, "this, you can have it".

"Well, umm, no. I actually do not want it that way. I wished to snatch it."

"Ok. But, you can have it."

"I do not want it anymore. Thank you"

I left the place and better never return to this culture.

The damage continues to transfer unless someone heals.

The Magical Coin

The first part of my journey was a numismatist searching and collecting old coins from different parts of the country. It was fun scanning the local areas and outskirts of the city for rare coins.

This is how I met most of the legends.

In this search, I met many other collectors, some of them searching for magical objects, coins, plants, etc. As a kid, it was interesting to listen to all folk legends about coins with magical powers.

One such coin was said to have pictures of Indian gods and a depiction of Ramayana.

I found one of such coins in 2004 at a minimal price of 12-14 rupees (1 USD equals 40 Rupees).

Though the coin looks prehistoric, it was identified as Ramtanka, a temple token carried by pilgrims to worship during their travels. These were made more than 100 years back. Such coins did not have monetary value but were made for religious purposes.

Pictures

Ramtanka Coin - Metal Brass

Green Tourmaline -Handpicked Crystal from Sikkim

VI

Hyderabad

Ticked the number 1 on the list of parikramas. There are 107 more to go. PARIKRAMA is the process of going around the temple in one full circle with prayers and chantings.

This is the second time I have visited Chilkur Balaji in Hyderabad, also known as Visa Balaji. The temple is known for fulfilling wishes and primarily for getting Visa and hence the name.

This was a long day and not the easy one like any other tourist site. One hundred eight parikramas around a temple with a large area was an exhausting workout. I began at 11 AM and went upto 4 PM to complete the parikramas. This was a day filled with devotion, talks on mythologies, Indian temples, and why we go around in a particular direction.

The saint in the temple explained the concept of north and south poles and related science to go around the temple. There must be a reason hundreds of devotees do this in this temple.

My schoolmate accompanied me on this tour. It was his first visit, so he took only 11 parikramas and spent the day sitting under a tree where I walk in the sun and at times sit by his side gasping for breath.

There is something I wished to do, is travel the country and find the ancient texts that are said to have secret knowledge of medicine and spirituality.

Every time I visit places, I hope to find someone or something that will reveal the formulae. For now, I am counting on my parikramas and expecting to be blessed with some divine knowledge.

VII

Madurai

The days of our post-graduation, it was a weekend morning group of students visited Meenakshi temple.

This temple has a huge built structure with no count to the number of idols. It is said that this temple has idols of all the gods and goddesses known in India.

We entered the main gate of the temple and the inner gates to the main hall.

There were people around this tree with a metal fence. It seemed everyone was there to touch the tree. Someone said that tree must be touched to receive the blessings.

For some reason, people tried, but no one seemed to reach the tree. There was a fair distance between the tree and the boundary railing.

We did our turns, but there was more gap than it is possible to stretch.

I tried—no way to reach, tried again with full strength and then surrendered. There is no way the distance could be covered.

The third time was slow to go but consistent stretching. The shoulder passed the rail this time, which got stuck for the first two trials due to excess pressure. The harder one would push, the more stuck the shoulder gets between the metal rods. Only a slow, consistent stretch allows passing by the small space, and the hand could stretch longer than average.

After working through it for a minute, the tip of my finger touched the tree. And then I felt people touching my shoulder.

"You are blessed. Because you touched the tree, people also touched you as part of their blessings".

"Well, if the blessing flows like that!!!" smiles...

There was one clear message from this tree. One cannot reach the core of consciousness by force or strength, neither by not trying. And probably when you touch the core, you also induce others to become conscious.

I also realized a pattern of forcing myself in anything when I start and then give up, later doing it slowly and consistently.

VIII

Tanjavore

After a science conference in Tanjavore, it was time to explore the city. It is one of the most magnificent temples I had the chance to visit. I took some pictures inside the temple.

Nine years later, I found the pictures on my computer—one of them depicting an image of Shiva-ling with some design at the back. There were probably hundreds of such structures in this one temple. I had an interest in this particular sign because I have been coming across this one multiple times.

Asking multiple people about their views about the temples' designs and symbols, I realized these are not just artistic designs.

There was a time a spiritual master would create a design and meditate on it for their entire lifetime. This design would symbolize this spiritual person's ascendance and attainment in human life. Each symbol means a spiritual master's work and sacred blessings in that site. The path of discipleship from a master is followed by this one unique symbol.

I had the chance to meet disciples from different spiritual sects. Some of them wear pendants with specific designs as a sign of their spiritual lineage. The disciples value the symbol more than anything in their spiritual and mundane life.

Being able to connect to any such sacred design means receiving blessings from the spiritual master.

This concept was left to a theory because there was no further information received.

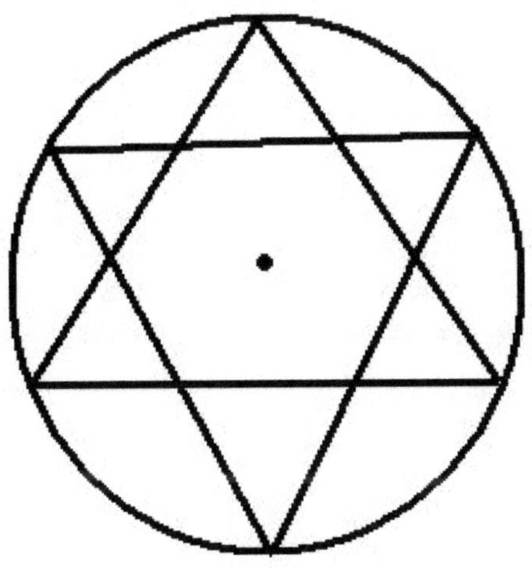

Design from Tanjavore

IX
Chennai

Another symbol that took my attention was in a temple in Chennai.

I was waiting for others to at the gate of this temple when my feet itched so bad that I began rubbing my feet against the floor. It was a rough rock and feels good to itch. But I felt something more coarse under my feet. I looked down, and there was a design on the floor; a triangle with three waves like an artistic design for a window depicting the airflow.

I kept a note of the design to enquire later. Which never happened.

I met so many symbols in the writing journey that it was impossible even to remember them.

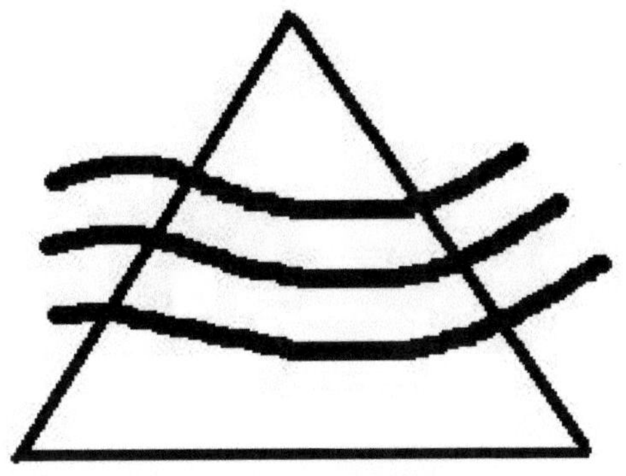

Chennai Temple

Meditation Symbol from Kanyakumari

Design found in Every Temple

Recreation of a design found in almost every temple in India. A similar design was found on a wall hanging decor used for meditation. The focus of meditation is said to be the central dot.

X

Healing Symbols

I caught a pink eye infection which later turned hemorrhagic, causing the eyes to bulge and blood red. It took two weeks to recover from the condition, but the bloodshot marks seem not dissolving.

Someone was inquiring about yoga and meditation classes in Kolkata, and I received a contact about a healing class. This was not the time I had any idea about healing systems.

There was hope for relief from the blood clots marks, so I decided to join the other person to attend the weekend session.

It helped. The large blood clot seemed to dissolve at the end of this class. The following day I found it less than half. Now I could walk around without glasses and not scaring people.

The second level of this healing system shared multiple Japanese words as healing symbols. This was the first time I realized what I was writing about.

The class was about Usui reiki system.

Later that year, I began writing and sharing pieces of my work, whereby I had the chance to interact with a number of other authors, healers, and coaches. In this time, I learned about a vast different spectrum of concepts from around the world.

The first Energy Healing

One health problem that I developed during my graduate years and went worse at the beginning of doctorate research. A burning inflammation under the left foot that reaches upto the left shoulder. I was under various treatments and therapies for years but with not much relief.

It felt like a lump of burning coal was placed under feet, and the heat radiates upwards. I already tried all the therapies and household measures people recommended then decided to give up.

There was a page I was reading on scientific experiments with a healing system, then found a healer offering a healing session for 60 euro with a trial session for free.

No loss in trying out a healing.

The appointment and time was fixed via mail, and I was ready that night to experience the first energy healing ever. I already read what was online, and it sounds like a scam or out-of-world concept. It is relatively impossible concept.

The session began close to midnight, and I was expecting to witness something.

I did experience what was to change my path of research.

A feeling of static electricity sparking under the left feet, and then my ankle moved 2-3 times to release the stress on the facia and arch. The electric feeling ran through the feet towards the body and bypassed the shoulder, and moved to the right side of my head.

There was a lot of pricking and movements on the right of the head as if a medical procedure and stitches were done. The next moment I remembered the reason for the pain. 2005 it was after one of the exams I had an accident and later woke up in bed. I do not remember the accident and the reason for the injury on the right side of the head. This later developed as neural pain on the left side of my body.

The next morning I woke up and found the hard spot under my feet has disappeared, and the burning pain was gone like it never existed.

A world of multidimensional possibilities in medical research stood right in front of my face. If not for a direct experience, it was impossible to believe.

This intensified my urge to study ancient healing techniques.

After a couple of years studying all available tools and techniques, I finally met the founder of the healing system in Mumbai. I also experienced an advanced healing process with the team. By the time I returned to Kolkata, my urge to learn energy healing totally vanished. For some reason, I did not feel like going any further. It was a Healing for the need of Healing.

I moved on to the next thing, Human behavior, and psychology. The doctor I had been consulting with for years named the healing experience as mesmerism, which led me to find a teacher in hypnotherapy and move to all other therapies in psychology.

Neurolinguistics

It was a hectic time working on lab experiments and also presenting research papers. What I always felt was a gap of skills being on stage. The first NLP workshop I attended was with the idea of professional coaching. I believed it was about being confident on stage.

During the later part of my writing, someone commented on my writings that the temple designs have to do with Neurolinguistics symbols. There was no further information available, and advanced NLP is not something affordable to everyone.

I borrowed some money from my lab mate and booked the next upcoming workshop in Kolkata.

I was expecting to discover the core concept of the designs.

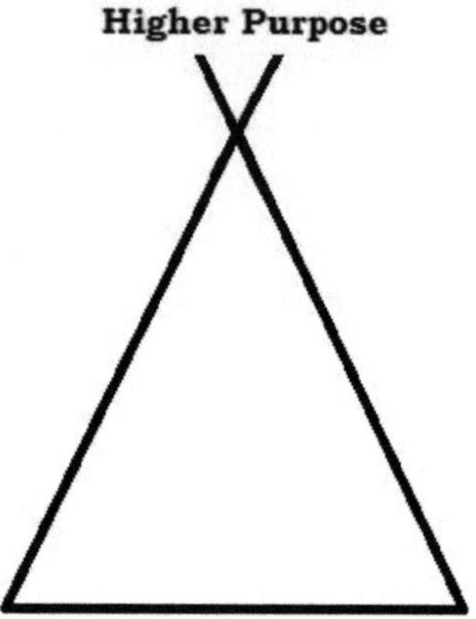

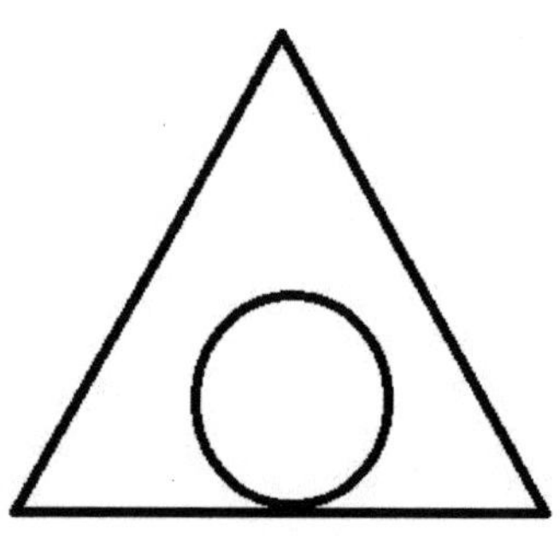

Judgements

Multilevel Alignment

Rituals help in focusing the inner resources

XI

Tirupati

Those were the days of post-graduation. After the evening football match in the PhD hostel, I was with one of my friends from the telecommunication department taking tea. It was him who would always strike a conversation about the great places to visit.

"My brother visited Tirupati a few years back."

“I know Tirupati is a great place, but it is far from Madurai, somewhere in Andhra.”

“It is not far. Just overnight”.

“That is not far. It is Friday evening. If there is just one friend to get along with. I am all packed and ready”.

“What!!!”

There has been some confusion for few minutes and complete silence.

“You like that type of last-minute plan!”

In half an hour, he returned with his college bag, ready for the tour.

That was a sporty attitude.

I realized one thing, though. Life is all about one friend who is always ready to get along.

We hardly had any directions till we reached the railway station.

There was a night train to Chennai. He got all directions to Tirupati from his dad on the way.

After the call, he was silent and tried not to make faces.

"Dad said, donate your hairs in Tirupati".

"Yes, I heard from many that it is a blessing to be able to do that."

"I wish to do so. But then we need to return to University."

"Hmm. We have overnight to think."

Early morning we reached Chennai and then took a bus to CMD. After that, getting refreshed and grabbing breakfast, we got our bus to Thirumala.

It was about 11 AM we reached THIRUMALA from where we were to walk 3500 steps and about 20 kms to reach the temple.

We got our footwear in the bag, washed our hands and feet in the flowing water at the entrance steps, and started walking bare feet.

It was 8 hrs of walking and climbing through the mountain. All the way, we talked about everything in life. Especially about our wish to be there at Tirupati.

"One of our seniors told a story that Tirupati is blessed, and you won't get sore feet after walking for hours."

"Such is the power of devotion and the blessings of Tirupati Maharaj".

Around 7:30, we reached the first gate for the pilgrims who come walking. The gates pass close by windows where we got soap and half a piece of a razor blade.

We smiled at each other.

"Stop thinking."

As we entered the hall, it was the place to donate hairs and take a bath.

We took our turns in guarding our bags and being under the razor.

And then it happened.

I lost control.

It took a peak in my head and flowed like a drug in my body.

A wave of bliss. My head was all light, and a strong sense of happiness flowing. And it radiates.

The Joy of Beingness.

I started to giggle at my friend. Both are now unrecognizable after losing hair. Neither could I recognize my existence. It was there and not. This is the first time I experienced bliss by losing myself. The states of bliss continued for another week or so. Then I had to struggle seeking it. Finally, it eluded away and back to our daily life.

I just wished never to return.

Back to where we were. After bathing at this place, we prepared for the darshan – temple visit.

The way was through the market as we tried to peek into every shop on the streets. It was halfway near the temple, and it began to rain.

Ready for the temple visit that night, we realized there was a policeman we met on the way trying to explain something; we forgot the temple entry passes. And now will have to wait for 12-24 hours to get entry.

But there is no going back.

We joined the general pilgrim line got to the inner hall where we were supposed to wait for hours.

I cannot relate to time or anything happening around me. The bliss has taken over, and everything seemed in perfect harmony. I had no problem with anything or anyone.

We made friends with other pilgrims. Many happy beings discussing over the small tube of toothpaste snicked in through the security and about the Prasadam, the only food available inside the hall.

After 2 hrs, the main gate opened, and we were finally there. We were visiting our dream place.

It was only for a moment to get a glimpse of Tirupati Maharaj, and then the crowd pushed us out.

We decided to stay in the pilgrim center that night but then got on a bus to leave this place.

While I remember the feeling, I could not find it again for years. There was no clear expression of that state.

A Powerful transformation

About eight years passed when I got another chance to visit Tirupati. This time being in that place has been altogether different than the first time.

A lot has changed in the past few years, and since the sickness in 2016, I turned all the more sensitive to spiritual essence.

A much intense experience this time. So intense that I must have been high and lost for 10-20 minutes when I sat to rest inside the temple. The place vibrating, my ears ringing, the chantings of the mantras in the entire space, the sacred writings on the walls, and an intense level of spiritual energy flow. Someone later made a comment, "You have turned into a transformer and emit a strong field around."

But there was much more than that. Did I sleep while sitting on the stairs?

I realized from this place that the sacred sites are connected to the masses at the spiritual level. These places also serve as a direct connection with the universal level of spiritual energy from which the human is otherwise disconnected.

The temple designs and work of the past yogis create the sacred sites so that the upcoming world continues to have the connection.

But why is it that only some people experience it? There must be clear answer to this. And if the theories are true, the spiritual energy must be felt by everyone.

Do we need to have special antennae to experience that?

XII

Mayapur

It was Saturday morning, and my cousin offered to take us on tour to a new place. I did not know where we were to travel.

It was already noon we got on the train and reached the destination railway station after four hours of journey. There is more to go before we reach the spot. About an hour in auto-rickshaw, we reached the ghat then crossed the river on a boat.

As soon I reached the other side of the river, there was a phenomenal change in consciousness. I was there and not at the same time. The intensity went high enough to make me feel totally drained and all confused.

This never happened to me before. It was for the first time witnessing the intense spiritual field of a place. Something that created the change in awareness all I need was a place to sit and absorb in the moment.

We took a rickshaw and asked the driver to take us to the last visiting spot. Because it is already evening, we need to return to the railway station for the train at 8 PM.

This place has 6-8 places to visit, and we hardly had 3 hours in hand. The rickshaw driver took us to the first place as most important to visit. This was the birthplace of Chaitanya Mahaprabhu, the great spiritual teacher in our place. Our ancestors were disciples of this great teacher.

I could not resist the urge to sit silently for a long time. There were no words to describe the intensity of this place. It was always annoying not to express what is happening while others hurry to travel the place. People tend to be more annoying while this intensity goes to a level of inner suffering. I could not help but disengage from others and allow them to travel while I stay alone.

There is no way to express what I was experiencing. A type of ungroundedness and feeling lost, intensity of anger, then ecstatic bliss flowing for a long time. There was no memory of time. I do not know what it was. There was no way to identify.

As the energy integrated, it felt like I am back. Totally grounded, refreshed and ready to travel. But it was already time for the train.

For me, this was not a usual tour. I did not visit the tourist spots nor had time to witness the sunset. There were only silent comments about how I ruin a trip. But I had no way to describe it.

All I could do is hope for the day people understand. Or atleast I understand what happens.

Months later, there was another tour. This time there was no such experience of ungroundedness. I had all the time to travel and visit places.

That afternoon we crossed the river and headed to another spot when an old lady came forward and offered a tilak (mark or design made on the forehead as a religious/ spiritual sign). The material was white and probably formed of sandalwood and some chalk. It is the culture of this place to draw this special design from the tip of the nose to the top of the forehead. There was a pleasant aroma in the material used. The lady took a small amount of money as a donation and left.

Now we were travelling by boat to another site. And I was all focused on the tip of my nose. It felt funny to wear that tilak.

And then there was a cool wave on my face, not like the usual breeze.

There was a continuous flow near the tip of the nose or the site where the symbol was drawn. In the years of travelling and having spiritual experiences, I had learnt to ignore things at times and continue with the normal.

But the process has its flow.

Mayapur has made the major shift in the past two visits. It probably took few months to integrate the energy shifts received from this place.

Finally, when it was time to write this chapter there was a pure expression of the experience.

"The site of ego could be replaced with Devotion".

This entire journey and shift was named **Chaitanya Kriya**; the ability to release ego and replace it with devotion.

These words later formed the key to connecting to the process.

Food has essence

It was dinner time, and I searched for hotels when someone directed me to collect dinner coupons served by the temple. For a small price, one gets to eat as much as one needs.

Few hundred pilgrims were inside the hall waiting to get served. What caught my attention was a huge picture of Krishna and his friends sharing food. There was a divine feeling being in this place.

The afternoon lunch was on the roadside hotel, and I hardly could swallow anything. Now the aroma of food and the divine bliss flows together.

What was different about the food was beyond a mixture of ingredients. It was delicious and had something I could not point out. There is something else that is beyond the five senses.

Two chapattis and some rice were enough to fill my stomach, but then it reached my heart. A deep content with food was a rare experience.

I later enquired about it to a shop where I received an answer that directed me further into the yogic path.

This food has devotion to God. It was prepared as prasadam and, after being offered to God, served to all pilgrims.

No doubt it brings great content in the heart.

Chanting to Healing code

I practised chanting meditation for my entire life and have been doing so every day. But I hardly experienced any effect that people talk about. Except for feeling calm and focused, there was nothing further.

I was enquiring this in my mind when it happened in total clarity. It was a night of Janmashtami I realized the meaning. The next few days or few weeks were transformational.

Krishna is the highest of all forms. The chant 'Hare Krishna' means everyone is Krishna. But after chanting a thousand times in meditation when I treat others anything less than Krishna, the chanting turns into a lie. It will have no effect.

This was an overwhelming experience, and the depth of meditation shifted such deep that it took hours to few days to integrate the energy. Everything has transformed in a moment.

Years later, when I talk of the concept and the meaning of chant, it could cause a similar transformational effect in anyone who connects with the concept.

This was the first concept of Placebo Codes. Words spoken from the depth of self-realization has a strong effect on the self or anyone else listening.

Effect of Chantings

Chantings reach and continue to work at the level of philosophy of life. The mind continues to apply it in every moment and every aspect of life.

Healing with Mantras

Healing with mantras or other holistic systems affects Philosophy of Life's level (Values, Sense of Self, Purpose and Higher Purpose). The transformation in these levels creates the embodiment of a new healthy self which shows up as a shift in consciousness, behaviour and patterns. The positive changes also release the stress and adverse effects caused by harmful internal programs creating the curative response.

Philosophy of Life
Healing
Goal
Self
Beliefs
Skills
Actions
Environment

XIII

Benarus - The city of Shiva

It was 4 AM I reached the Varanasi railway station. I was to stay in this city for two days with one of our former lab trainees.

Mushroom Incubation

His room was no less than a mushroom incubation centre. There was fungus growing everywhere.

"If I touch anything here, I am afraid to get a fungal infection".

He giggles, "Sir, this will strengthen your immunity".

I had no other option but to stay with him, trying as safe to not get in touch with anything.

There was never a second chance I saw another boys hostel this dirty.

Only Baba Saves me now.

Salvation at Ganga ghat

That evening we spent time at the sacred ghat of river Ganga. It is said that the Soul is purified of all karma and breaks the cycle of life and death in this place.

On the way to benaras there was tragic news of a family friend losing his life to an accident. The saint asked to release a candle and flowers in the river as prayers for the departed soul.

I smell like a Tree

The next morning, I had a meeting to present my work.

It was a long hour waiting for the trainee to complete his work.

Sitting on the wall outside, I felt something on my shoulder, and to my amazement, it was a squirrel. He/she seems calm around a human. Climbed my shoulder and shifted to another, then walked past my chest. For few minutes, it stayed on me and then left for the nearby tree.

This morning I used one of the imported deodorants gifted to the trainee from his girlfriend, and I now smell like wood or a tree.

Swollen Face

Half of my wisdom teeth went missing the night before when I began my journey to benaras. The dentist prescribed urgent surgery to remove the leftover to ease the pain and inflammation.

But, I had upcoming seminars and presentations in the following weeks.

If the tooth gets removed, I won't be able to talk for a week or two.

A pain killer and mouth wash prescription and now ready for the days' presentation.

Huge depository of Ancient Spiritual Work

This city is said to have a massive amount of spiritual knowledge at various places, groups and among the saints that inhabit the area. Secret formulas that only yogis know and some of them extracted for nanoparticle research to the grand texts that are a few thousand years old.

The Body pose creates a Resonance

Some of the works on yoga and mudra positions by an ancient yogi named Matsyamuni inspired the concept of Autoreflexor.

It was after reading the work on the walls, I realized specific mudras and yogic positions create a powerful shift in emotions and flow of energy.

The human body anchors emotions and consciousness through a subtle network similar to our neural signalling system. The yogic positions and mudras activate this system to refine and embody higher consciousness.

Sarnath

The next day we visited Sarnath, the place where Buddha took his first spiritual teachings. The huge garden with the ancient temple and a grand museum took an entire day.

The next site was Boddhagaya, the place where Buddha received enlightenment.

Soul and its Correction

With years spent writing, I learned that the source of all disease roots in the consciousness much earlier than it shows up in the body. It is through all layers of consciousness the choice was made that leads to the experience of sickness.

It would be only misleading the flow if the disease is removed without correcting the core issues (the choices that lead to the current state).

I studied multiple healing modalities, but I do not have a clear answer to correcting the core issue.

I had no idea how and what it means to correct the Soul.

Probably, it was Shiva's calling to the Ghat of Benaras.

My tour is complete, and I needed to leave Banaras the following day. Much of this tour was a failure for the book or even research opportunities.

I decided to do what I do the best. Cherish being in that place. The answer was there, but I was unable to point it out.

Salvation has a test

There was some forward in the social media group. The video was one of the spiritual gurus talking about the Shivas process of giving salvation in Varanasi.

The explanation was that a person would go through an entire lifetime of experiences and karma in few moments, and those who purify through it will receive salvation.

So Shiva has a way of Soul correction, a space where the soul would experience all the lifetimes of karma and integrate the lessons.

But only Shiva knows how to do it!

It took few years before this knowledge became a system that could spontaneously correct human behaviour, perception, attitude, patterns, and other types of consciousness distortions.

'**Soul correction**' was a blessing from Shiva.

(soul correction code is shared in the book Beyond Placebo. used for behavioral corrections)

XIV
Boddhagaya

The day was hectic, and trains were overcrowded. I missed the morning train because there was no way to get in the coach. The next train had a similar problem, but the reservation coaches had space to get in. I paid a fine to the TTE and got a seat to Gaya station.

It was already afternoon when I reached Gaya. I had only a few hours in this city as I need to catch the train at 7 PM. Travelling to the main site took almost an hour, and I realized it is impossible for me to get back in time. There needed to be a change in plan.

The main site in Boddhagaya was the tree under which Buddha got enlightenment. I needed to leave back all electronics before getting inside. There were Buddhist monks everywhere. Walking past the main temple, I reached the site around the tree where groups of monks were meditating. Generally, I am pretty sensitive to these places. The vibrations of the space sometimes take over long before reaching the site.

This place was quite gentle. No energetic overloads. It was just normal and well worth spending time doing nothing. I watched the monks doing their practice.

The Path of Boddhisatva

The one who took so much pain and suffering to bring a path of salvation to all is a true Bodhisattva. There is no greater service.

There was no time in hand, I had to rush, but the train departed before reaching the railway station.

The other option was taking a bus.

Covid Pandemic

I kept busy with my thesis work for some time. I also got the book contract with a publisher and had few months to submit the assignment. Meanwhile, I mailed people to send their reviews.

I was planning to travel towards the north this time. But then the pandemic was announced, and the time ahead seems challenging.

It delayed the degree award. The computer got damaged, and few months passed waiting to get back to writing. The website created expired and needed upgrades.

Among all this, the first book was completed and released in Dec 2020.

XV

Identifying the hidden Programs

"There is a core motivation behind every act."

A lot has happened in the past few years after this project started. Metaphorically, I was a balloon blown up to its capacity, and all I needed was to pop.

It happened as the debris of past programs purged in this journey.

I realized the recent experiences had been a replay or a complex level of past experiences. At the same time, I had the choice to continue or step out of the programs.

These are some of the chosen stories and events that were identified with my hidden core values. Not a single of these programs was a personal choice. They just happened to be information picked from others.

The stories might help the readers relate to personal choices and repeating patterns they would like to get rid of.

The stories are expressed as personal narratives in the form of a self-healing session or inner work (allows surfacing layers of internal programs). At times the description might seem broken or disconnected as it is a memory surfacing in a session.

Treated like a Dog

Someone just called me a dog. Being treated like a stray dog has taken on my nerves.

I wished it to stop once and for all.

These were the days I was training with a senior psychiatrist in medical hypnosis and autosuggestion techniques. We use to practice autosuggestion and deep relaxation in class every weekend.

I also continued to practice after the classes. Most times, my focus was to work with stage fright. But this evening, the bad feeling lingered to the session.

I wished to know the reason for the treatment. And the mind began to lift the veils.

The entire experience:

I was with my classmate on his bike. We were already late for class.

It was 10 minutes late when we stood at the door of the class. We asked for permission, and there was no reply.

"Stand there".

So we were to be punished for getting late!

There were others standing in the corner. Such a relief to be able to share the punishment!

But it was something else going on.

I remembered the words, "you will be treated as Stray dogs, and no one cares even if you are .....".

A wave of rage took over, and the muscles tightened, fist clenched as a tear dropped from the corner of eye.

It is over now, as I woke up from the session.

This was one of my own successful regressions and the gift to look behind the veils of mental structures.

Structure of Reality (shared in the first book) was one of the most powerful codes that helped many become aware of their mental programming that negatively influences their lives.

The mind does not have filters or guards while interacting with the world, neither it cares. It would copy anything and everything and keep applying to your perception of reality.

Being able to shift past this programming takes great inner strength. Only a few do that in life, while most live as victims of programs that are not their own.

The one who experiences this reality is not the Self; it is the Sense of Self developed over life experiences. And it is deeply damaged and scarred.

The only path is stepping past the Sense of Self and then restructuring the entire Self.

Self Realization is knowing you are in control of your Reality.

Meeting the Real Ghost

It was 2 AM I closed my computer and switched off the lights, and preparing for sleep.

Through the window, I saw something moving past the nearby farmland and it disappeared. I tried a closer look, but it was gone.

Another moment I was fright-struck. There is no one in my room or the hall. What am I supposed to do?

For another few minutes, "I should have stayed in the city."

This is my village home, and it is for the first time I am here for an extended stay.

Now I wished to move.

When I collected enough strength, I wished for the body response to clear. It took another minute, and then I am ready to clear it off.

The perception was to be uprooted.

And the feeling tucked to its source!

My granny use to tell this story when we were kids, and I use to feel this same fright when listening to her.

I just had a recap of the story because all the stories belonged to this place, and the situation was perfect.

Probably, my mind does not like this place.

I just met the Ghost.

Mind will do anything if it gets bored.

Fear of the dark is a sign of boredom and inactivity. In such a case, the mind will play any old reel stored inside to bring in some activity.

If the mind is afraid of something?

Most probably, a damaged Human form frights the mind because it tends to mirror.

Rejection is another emotion that triggers fear. It covers everything from stage fear to failures in life.

If a fear eludes the sense of self, then it is rooted in childhood experiences.

Stories do a lot of inner programming than anything else.

Inner Critic to Inner Mentor

I am extremely critical and judgemental towards others. At the same time, I had such a strong inner critique that it takes me few days to complete a work that otherwise would take few hours.

I was working on this structure. And I was there right where it started:

My notebook was on the floor. The teacher did not like my writing on the topic.

"What a non-sense writing. even school kids do better than you. In such a case, you will not pass this exam".

I didn't pass the exam because I would better not study than to face this abuse every day.

When I look back on the topic, it showed up to be a silly concept. Only if the teacher must have left me undisturbed, I must have completed the subject in an hour. But, what he did left a mark and a harsh inner critic.

Now, I wish to delete this abusive teacher and be a mentor to myself—one who would accept my current skills and then adds what is needed to refine them.

I wish for a mentor to refine the qualities and awaken what I already have to its mastery level. I ask for the creation and skills of such a mentor now.

Over the years, I realized the dense sabotage dissolved. And I turned out to be a mentor to others.

The inner mentor has been Awakened.

Dukhendu

In graduation years, I received a pet name from seniors; 'Dukhendu'-who is always sad/ one who brings sadness.

This was not my nature, but I was helpless. I felt drained out all the time. Years have passed in the struggle to get back to a happy flow.

As we graduated out and moved to universities, I found a major reason for my situation.

The only difference between our graduation life and post-graduation lifestyle was morning breakfast. In graduate college, I hardly focused on morning breakfast and probably use to take lunch at 2 PM at times after 4.

This was a distressful and nerve-breaking habit. The effect of stressful days took years to surface.

The major problems were realized after my doctorate as I moved into writing in this project. Only if I had focused on it back then, years of suffering must have been avoided.

In case life doesn't seem to go well, take a ritual/habit of self-care and proper nourishment in whatever situation. If there are other issues underneath, they would surface and will be easy to manage.

Note: It is impossible to face difficulties (complex work needing refined skills) with a starving body and mind.

A parched and starving body has more need to relief creating agents causing addictions.

A powerful self-care technique was taught in reiki healing classes - the 24 points self-healing.

This one technique for 21 days duration heals years of stress and other related problems.

Malific Dialogues / philosophies

"A girl can destroy as many lives to find her Mr. Perfect".

She was sitting on the other side giving her lectures. I did not realize this would get imprinted and create a life of distrust and chaos in relationships. There was no reason as to why the mind would copy such nonsense.

Life would have been much better, only if the Mind listens and answers to the owner.

If astrology is manipulation

I had this pain and inflammation on my left side all these years. When working with the hypnosis relaxation technique, I worked to relax the muscles feeling the pain.

The layers of memories with the pain shifting intensity:

That feeling I remember is so clear now. He was holding my hand and said, "You will always have stomach issues and pain on the left side of the body. There are signs of upcoming failure and dishonor. Stay away from ....., wear this ruby.....blah blah "

We just completed our class 10 exams. Now everyone has to choose the next level.

It was interesting to know some of the neigbour met this renowned astrologer to find what would be best for them. So we decided to give it a try.

Things were all metaphoric. But in the later two years, life brought all types of bad events that continued for later many years.

The damage was seeded in the core adolescent mind.

Accumulated problems ooze out

I just got thrown out of a job I had trained for three months. There was a legal issue and has to go through a meeting with the company lawyers. None was my fault, but someone was to be responsible for the problem.

Sometimes later, an accident happened, and I burned both my hands. Then I had already failed the exams. Now there was no chance of earning or even getting admission to a university.

Luck changes any moment

The college stairs. A senior's lunchbox in my hand, and I was busy munching on the food.

At a distance, these two post-graduate seniors were in discussion among themselves. It is a national entrance test they were discussing.

"I had seen the question paper, and I felt I know most of the answers. Only if I had prepared for three months, I must have cracked this exam. I know you can do it easily".

I do not know how and when it hit the core.

A few days later, I found myself getting all question papers and checking them out.

And taking a look at the calendar. 'I have fair enough time.'

There were people who would often show up and make negative gestures to the papers. But the program has gone in the right place, and I was decided to protect it.

Everything changed with that one choice.

Growing beyond astrology

If there is a possibility to grow beyond astrological influences and change your luck?

The answer from people: there is no way to do that. The position of planets decides the life of a person, and a person has to go through the process.

But, there is something that might change the laws. A spiritual initiate who would grow past the planets and solar system template would be free from the influence.

That made no practical sense to grow past planets. Does that mean leaving the solar system?

Spiritual concepts collected over time explained it on a behavioral level. Mastering the attributes of all 12 sun signs, a person would be able to grow spiritually beyond the influence of the astrological influence.

So, one sun sign would be me, and there must be 11 other levels of masters to learn from.

Non-sense!!!

Align with 12 Sun Signs

Years passed as I realized astrology is developed on identifying a certain set of fixed behavior patterns in the population.

Humanity has only a few archetypes behaviour patterns that govern their lives. The interaction with others creates the interaction structure of learning and growing.

Planets were brought in the equation to keep a universal form of presentation: a Witness to the Structures.

The concept of Inner dragon

(The name was a random choice of metaphor. Do not relate to already known dragon healing or reiki systems.)

This is the second time I have met the concept of spiritual attacks that damaged a person's body. I do not personally believe in the idea because the core yogic philosophies believe all experiences as the creation of self.

This concept provides great inner power over your life experiences. But the story of this person sounds different.

The cultural and spiritual beliefs were different from Indian yogic systems, and there is no sure way to point out the differences.

2- 3 days passed, working on the two concepts to meet a corrective point. I need proof that would correct both the beliefs and the physical damage.

This is one of the first works of metaphoric analysis and reversing somatic response.

Suppose there is damage from a spiritual attack. In that case, it could be a sign of strong self-sabotage or self-destruction triggered in the emotions. The outside is just a reflection.

I wish to develop a system to align all inner resources so that triggers of emotions or even strong choices to cause damage would be defended. The most potent spiritual forces (inner resources) that control the path of experience and are known to be in the spine of a human being.

Indian yogic systems called it Kundalini or Serpent, while the Zen called it the Dragon.

After hours of inner reflection, the Inner Dragon awakened a Universal force that was called forth to help and protect a seeker from any possible damage in the path of Self Realization.

The first time the concept was shared, the person has shown a significant level of changes that appeared to reverse the physical damage caused due to the attack.

This concept later helped many seekers from falling into traps that would otherwise keep them stuck for years.

Color affects the mind

There was a direct experience as to how color affects mental and emotional states. The colors and their combinations could be used in more subtle levels of inner work.

It was during the creation of the color visualization series I had certain vivid and intense experiences.

The first was the creation of red color meditation video. The videos had red colors with flames to assist during meditation. One needs to look at the video for a minute and then continue visualizing the color for few minutes.

After the creation of the video, I left for a walk to the local market. For some reason, I had a constant feeling of threat/panic walking on the road. I tried to walk as much to the edge of the road as to keep a safe distance from vehicles. The peak of fear state continued as long as I did not return to my room. That night I realized this is how red color affects the mind. It does both i.e., making one afraid or feel strong. I was experiencing a tuning effect. A person high on red color might develop tendencies to control others while low on red color makes the person feel afraid.

The second experience was with bright white color with a tinge of purple. It was named platinum violet flames. This experience happened the following morning after the creation of the meditation video. I was walking past a building when I noticed the melodious sound of pigeons on the roof. There must be dozens of pigeons in that place. While I pass this place every day, I was experiencing some major differences at this moment. It was a deep joy in the songs of the pigeon that I did not pay attention.

This color combination is said to be the color of purification and joy. What it did was clear the mental fuss and stress of a busy life to feel lively in nature.

XVI

I Am and I Am not Experiment

Who Am I?

It was during a timeline walk technique I realized something about myself.

A large aspect of me and my world is a map of dedicated Numismatist. At the same time every time I wish to walk ahead the pull and weight I feel was also that of numismatic collection.

I map this city to the original map of what I use to find old and rare coins. It is same everywhere.

Now I feel blocked and weighted down by the same thing.

I wished to move ahead.

So, I made the decision and put down the weight. I do not have any purpose with the numismatist collections any more.

Later, I donated the foreign coins album, gifted the highest price coins and sold off other things. Decided to stop collecting.

The map crashed.

Who am I?

I AM not a numismatist. I was inspired by others to be collecting coins.

Who Am I now?

I am a researcher. I am here to experiment and create new information.

Class 3, I was appreciated for collecting a mimosa plant, "You will be a scientist someday".

I liked being appreciated. I put the mimosa plant back. I chose to leave and go further.

Who am I now?

I Am....

(Confusion and anger)

There is only darkness.

I am no one.

Nothingness

XVII

The Three sessions to Enlightenment

The subsequent three activations cover the complete template of enlightenment in Indian yogic systems. Among the seven levels of self-realization, the sixth forms the complete process of purification, testing and actualization. All distortions in consciousness begin to fall off in this process. In yogic path, it is a process of 3-7 years.

The coaching system explains awakening as correction of values and self then embodying the higher purpose through all aspects of life. This is called Self Actualization; becoming aware of who you are.

The spiritual system has the concept of God-realization, where the Self/ID/Ego dissolves and becomes one with higher values, consciousness and purpose. This structures the new sense of self.

Indian yogic systems have multiple tools and techniques shared over thousands of years that assist in the process of awakening. The later three activations cover the entire process.

The first dissolves the ego and its adverse effects, all sins, malice and diseases. The second activates the field of refined consciousness. At the third level, the Self dissolves and becomes one with the Source.

XVIII

Mantra that destroys all Sins

ॐ नमः शिवाय

This mantra is inscribed in every temple across India, but its fullness could be experienced when chanted in the sacred sites in the Himalayas. I had this intense and somewhat painful experience after chanting this mantra.

Once the emotions subsided, I realized it was a profound purging effect. Moreover, I also realized what a Sin is and how it is created. The purification revealed the layers through which negative experiences were created in life.

This mantra destroys malice, purifies the soul and clears the body of all diseases. It is also said to heal mental illness and personality disorders. On the emotional scale (shared in the first book), generally, it is rare for spiritual healing systems to affect the dark matrix range of emotions where personality disorders develop.

During the purging experience after chanting the Shiva mantra, I had certain experiences. Though it caused emotional pain, it has revealed the layer of behaviour that creates a negative experience.

For the readers, the mantra is written in english with proper pronunciation. The chanting is done only once for the first time initiation. Meditate or rest for some time after the mantra chant. Do not work with any other session for the time as it takes 1-2 days to integrate fully. Stay aware of any negative emotions and experiences (interactions) in this time, as it may direct you to the inner layers that created the life situations.

The correct pronunciation of the mantra:

Aum Namah Shivay

(In case the pronunciation feels incorrect, check for a mantra video with search OM NAMAH SHIVAY).

XIX

Multidimensional Continuum

This is a technique derived from 2000 years old sacred design carved on a copper plate.

There are multiple meditation techniques in Hinduism as well as in Buddhism that relates to this symbol. The meditation is practised by visualizing or gazing at the centre of the design.

Some theories say the symbol is a vibrational structure of the mantra OM. Some other theories call it the design of the soul.

Tapping into the multiple layers of the energy body needs activation of these layers through a process. Being able to activate and realign this structure opens up the natural flow of universal energies into the Body and the Individual's Energetic system.

Even if it seems to be a combination of triangles, the artist who was given the task to recreate a design for this book struggled for three days to point match the lines. After so many trials, the final design still has a mismatching point. For some reason, the calculations did not match the design and formations.

Importance

This activation has a significant effect on the mental, emotional and spiritual consciousness of a person. It is believed that the mind emits thoughts in the form of geometries and the emotions are denser manifestations of these geometric designs. Persons mental and emotional states are a collective of designs created in self and picked from around all through life.

Now, if a sacred geometry is applied to a person's field, it induces the energy field and all other geometries to align in the higher geometric field. This creates significant changes in mental and emotional states.

But when it comes to geometry like this, it applies a multilevel field of induction and creates a powerful resonance of changes in the entire consciousness.

This is more of the technical aspect of working with mudras, yogic positions and meditating inside a temple. It is directly activating the field on self.

Induction vs Permanent shift

Depending on the spiritual energy level of the initiate and the energy level applied, the effects could be partial induction or a permanent change.

A permanent shift happens if the person is ready to totally align with the resonance spectrum of the sacred design. In such a case, the person would change in no matter of time and at the same time make changes in everything interacted with.

How to receive

To activate the session, follow the process shared in the later part of the chapter. It is a meditation process for self, but it could be integrated into a healing session for others.

The first part of activation creates spin pulsation and warmth in the chakras and with energy flowing in the body. The later part of the process activates a chain reaction of energy work throughout the field and consciousness. The emotional purging experiences may happen during or after the session.

Allow atleast two weeks after the session to fully integrate the process. This phase goes through the surfacing of life experiences, perception, choices, and correction on all levels.

After the session

The session is an intense form of spiritual activation. The person needs a lot of rest after the session. Rest as much as needed, drink lots of water and stay aware of self in peace and joy. Avoid any drama or issues with others.

First Half of Session

The activation is worked in two halves, each lasting 15 to 20 minutes (the person receiving the session decides the time needed to rest). This session could be used as self-activation, or someone could act as a facilitator in the activation by working out the process on the client.

The first half is clearing and aligning the nine major chakras. The sequence for activation of the chakras is shown in the picture.

The activation is done with a design of a star. The upside design designates purification, upliftment and alignment with higher consciousness. The inverted triangle designates the embodiment of the purification process. The upside triangle is drawn first, followed by the inverted one. Each of the nine chakras receives this activation. Then the person must rest for 15-20 minutes (or as needed).

How to activate the design

The receiver must lie down comfortably and close eyes. Drawing the design means visualizing the design being drawn with a brush or finger (similar to drawing this design on sand). The design is made over each of the nine chakras in the sequence shown.

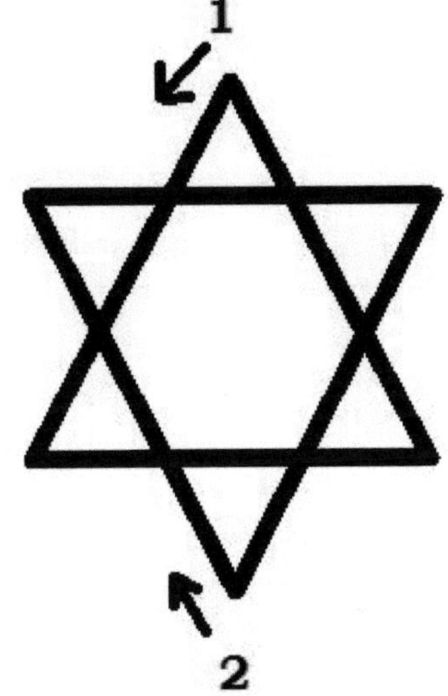

Chakra Alignment

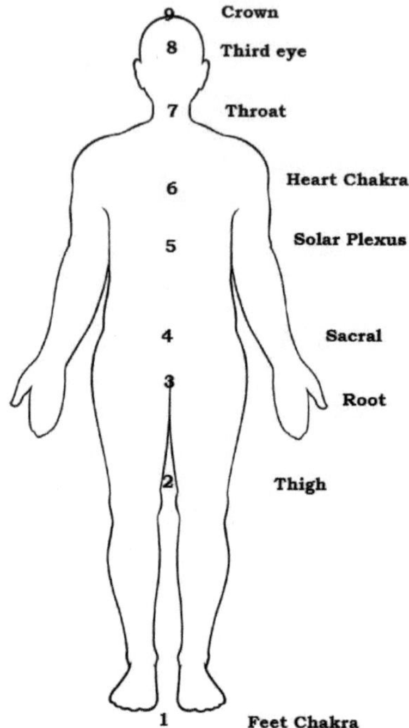

Nine Chakras

Second Half of the Session

The second half of the session is more complex than the first half because this has a total of 9 triangles in a particular sequence. The entire design is focused on the whole body and field of the person.

The design activates the layers of consciousness, aligning the self with higher consciousness.

Follow the sequence of triangles given, and it would reach this design ideally. There is no need to focus on the size of the triangles.

Multiple layers of Self

Start Drawing

The complete process has five steps. Follow the designs one by one.

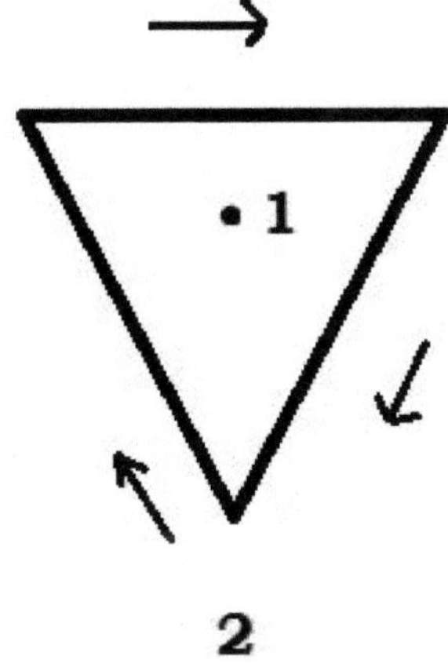

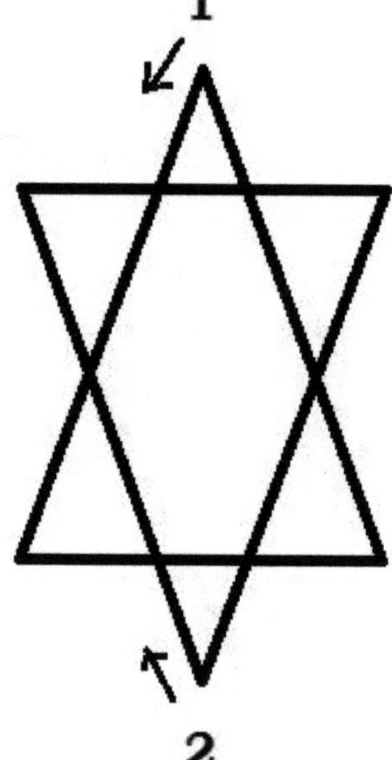
1
2

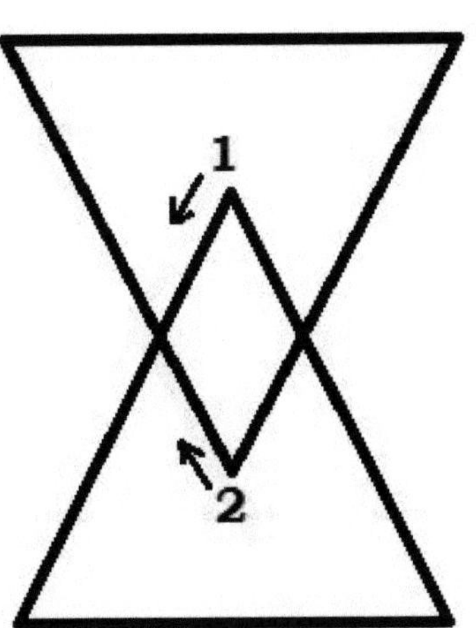
1
2

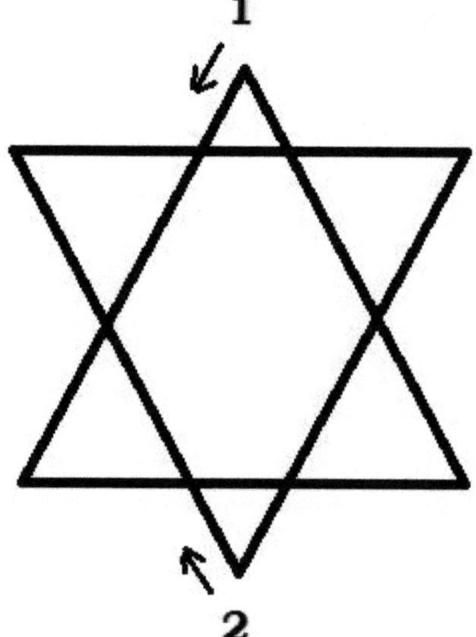
1
2

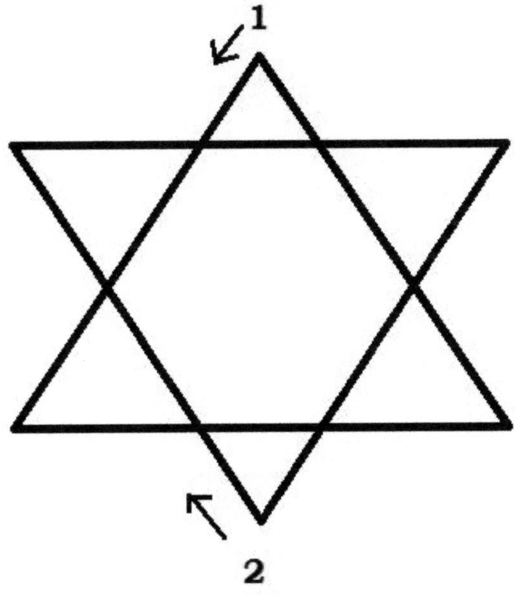

The design is complete. Rest for 15-20 minutes. Keep a gap of at least one week before working with the next session.

The complete design

XX

Reaching the depth of Meditation

Meditation on this code is similar to the healing codes shared in the first book. The session gives an experience of total Samadhi, the most profound state of meditation experienced. This state is said to transcend all dimensions of consciousness, and the self becomes absorbed in the source.

Once a Yogi experiences this state, it becomes one with the Sense of Self. A yogi might express this state in many ways:

"I Am the Source"

"I am both Yogi and Yog" (practitioner, process and the final outcome)

"I Am form and formless"

"I Am everything"

"Aham Brahmaswami"

"I Am always in meditation"

"I Am source of all knowledge"

What happens during the deep states

The most common experience is a total renewal in consciousness, the release of all stress and shift into total acceptance, change in mental, emotional states into grace.

The person reaches the source of consciousness and develops the awareness to step in or out of a life experience. There is the ability to dissolve any negative experience with acceptance. With time the yogi also develops unique skills and gifts needed in the path of service.

How to work with the session

Plan a weekend to work with the session. Commit to the purification of your body and mind. Work with the code as sleep meditation (works better when the body is deeply relaxed).

Read the code in mind, **" I Am Void"**

Close your eyes and relax. Allow the flow and sleep.

Following morning start your day with a cleansing bath and meditation. Keep the weekend free of any work. Allow all the emotions and experiences that surfaces.

There is no need to repeat the session.

XXI

A lifetime of Practice

"*Awakening is a nick in the fabric of Reality.*"

This is one of the simplest forms of meditation that anyone could follow. All it needs is silence and presence (presence does not mean focus but relaxed awareness).

Sit or lie down. Feel the stillness. Close your eyes and stay in that state.

All the levels and layers of consciousness align in this state. This is the Void or Universal state of Samadhi.

There is no better state of being.

Later Books

Book 3

Some of the spiritual teachers, healers and yogis after 2-3 decades of spiritual work gets stuck in this trap. This is one of the darkest side of spiritual work that only advanced yogis realize.

Medical conditions, emotional problems, legal lawsuits and all type of negative spiritual experiences that seem to have no solution hit the person. For now no one really knows what it is.

This book covers the topic based on direct interactions with some of the most advanced and dedicated spiritual practitioners who has to go through the inevitable test.

Book 4

An intensive form of yogic practice that covers all layers and levels of spiritual consciousness and transformation. This book shares the activation of a simple and powerful mudra that purifies and aligns a yogi in the most intense ways.

Book 5

This book shares cycle of ascension into 24 major activations shared with Placebo Codes. It completes the complete cycle of ascension/ purification and embodiment of the higher consciousness.

मैं अनंत हूं
मैं विभोर हूं
मैं शिव हूं

Printed by Libri Plureos GmbH in Hamburg,
Germany